Helping Children See Jesus

ISBN: 978-1-64104-050-1

Suffering
New Testament Volume 15: Acts Part 3

Author: Ruth B. Greiner
Illustrator: Frances H. Hertzler
Computer Graphic Artist: Ed Olson
Typesetting and Layout: Patricia Pope

© 2018 Bible Visuals International
PO Box 153, Akron, PA 17501-0153
Phone: (717) 859-1131
www.biblevisuals.org

All rights reserved. No part of this publication may be reproduced, stored in a retrieval system or transmitted in any form by any means, electronic, mechanical, photocopy, recording or otherwise, without the prior permission of the publisher, except as provided by USA copyright law.

RELATED ITEMS

To access related items (such as activities, memory verse posters and translated texts) please visit our web store at shop.biblevisuals.org and enter 1016 in the search box on the page.

FREE TEXT DOWNLOAD

To access a FREE printable copy of the teaching text (PDF format) in English or other available languages, enter S1016DL in the search box. Add the item to your cart, and use coupon code XTACSV17 at checkout. Once your order is processed you will receive an email with a link to the free download.

For I reckon that the sufferings of this present time are not worthy to be compared with the glory which shall be revealed in us. Romans 8:18

Lesson 1
PERSECUTION FOR CHRIST'S SAKE

NOTE TO THE TEACHER

When we studied about *The Church* (Volume 15), we learned of the triumphs of the first Christians as they took the Gospel to faraway places. One might suppose that, because of their obedience to the command of the Lord, the ministry was easy. Nothing could be farther from the truth! A careful study of the book of Acts might cause us to feel that the early Christians suffered one defeat after another. They were imprisoned in certain places, beaten, stoned, killed. (See, for example, what happened to just one of the early witnesses, Paul–2 Corinthians 11:23-27.) No matter what opposition they faced, the first century Christians obediently proclaimed the message of Christ. Their obedience involved suffering.

Someone has said that extraordinary afflictions are not always the punishment for extraordinary sins; sometimes they are the trial of extraordinary graces. God-given afflictions are spiritual promotions.

When Christians are in the perfect will of God are they allowed to suffer? Yes, according to the Word of God. However, it is encouraging to know that our problems (which are for only a short time) are winning for us a permanent and glorious reward. (See 2 Corinthians 4:17.) Whatever we may have to go through now is less than nothing compared to the magnificent future God has planned for us.

Scripture to be studied: Acts 3; 4:1-31; 1 Peter 2:19-20

The *aim* of the lesson: To show that sometimes God allows believers to suffer for doing good.

What your students should *know*: Suffering for Christ now is nothing compared to the glorious future God has planned for them.

What your students should *feel*: A willingness to suffer for Christ.

What your students should *do*: Be a bold witness (like Peter and John) this week before their friends.

Lesson outline (for the teacher's and students' notebooks):
1. The lame man begs (Acts 3:1-6).
2. The lame man has faith in Jesus and walks (Acts 3:7-26).
3. Peter and John imprisoned for preaching the Gospel (Acts 4:1-4).
4. Peter and John preach to the rulers, are threatened by them and continue preaching courageously (Acts 4:5-31).

The verse to be memorized:

For I reckon that the sufferings of this present time are not worthy to be compared with the glory which shall be revealed in us. (Romans 8:18)

THE LESSON

Have you ever been punished for doing something right? Have you ever been punished for doing something good?

Many years ago Peter and John, two of the apostles, were punished for doing something that was both right and good. Listen carefully as I tell you about it.

1. THE LAME MAN BEGS
Acts 3:1-6

The first Christians prayed together at the temple three times a day: nine o'clock in the morning, twelve o'clock noon and at three in the afternoon.

One afternoon Peter and John were on their way to the temple for the prayer meeting. At the Beautiful Gate of the temple they saw a poor lame man begging.

Show Illustration #1

The man held out his hands for money. Peter and John studied the man closely. "Look at us," Peter said. The lame man looked, expecting to receive money.

"I do not have any silver or gold," Peter continued, "but what I do have I will give to you."

The man must have thought to himself, *What can these men give me other than money? It is money that I need! Money!*

Then Peter added, "In the name of Jesus Christ, walk!"

How could he walk? He had never walked in his life.

2. THE LAME MAN HAS FAITH IN JESUS AND WALKS
Acts 3:7-26

Show Illustration #2

But Peter reached down, took him by the right hand and lifted him up. At once his feet and ankle bones were strong. He could walk! No longer would he have to sit beside the Beautiful Gate and beg. He would be able to work and earn money like other men.

He did not want to stay at the gate one moment longer. Do you think he hurried home to tell his family and friends the news? He did not! He walked right into the temple–and walked with legs that were well and strong. Peter and John were by his side, but they did not have to help him. Inside the temple the man who was healed leaped about and praised God for the wonderful miracle that had happened to him.

People turned to look at this man who was acting so strangely. They had seen him many times at the Beautiful Gate. They had heard him beg for money. They were astonished to see him walking and jumping and praising God.

Word of the miracle spread through the temple court. People crowded around to see the healed man and Peter and John.

Peter knew that the people were puzzled and that they wondered how the man had been healed. So he addressed the crowd: "Men of Israel, why are you so astonished at this? And why do you stare at us as though we made this man walk by our own power or goodness? It is God who has brought glory to His Son Jesus by doing this. Jesus was the One whom you rejected in the presence of Pilate. So you killed Jesus, the Prince of Life. But God raised Him from the dead. This man has faith in Jesus and

Jesus, by His power, has healed him and made him strong. You, too, should turn to Jesus so that your sins will be wiped out."

3. PETER AND JOHN IMPRISONED FOR PREACHING THE GOSPEL
Acts 4:1-4

Peter went on preaching. As he spoke the priests and the captain of the temple guard and the Sadducees came near to listen. (The Sadducees were Jews who did not believe in angels, spirits, the resurrection, nor did they believe in miracles.)

As they all listened to Peter they became angry. He was teaching the listeners the very things which they did not believe. They especially hated what Peter said about Jesus Christ's being raised from the dead.

Finally they could stand it no longer. Angrily they pushed their way through the crowd. They grabbed Peter and John and locked them up in jail for the night.

Show Illustration #3

Did Peter and John rave and shout to get out? No, indeed! They leaned against the prison walls and went to sleep!

What about those who had listened to Peter? Something happened in the hearts of many of them. They believed in Jesus Christ and were saved. They were new members of His Church, having been born into the family of God. Now there were about 5,000 men who belonged to the Lord Jesus Christ.

Peter and John had been doing what the Lord Jesus wanted them to do. They had been His witnesses, telling all who listened about His death and resurrection exactly as He had commanded them to do. And what had happened? They had been thrown into prison. How could this be? Why should they suffer for doing something good–something which Jesus Himself had ordered them to do?

4. PETER AND JOHN PREACH TO THE RULERS, ARE THREATENED BY THEM, AND CONTINUE PREACHING COURAGEOUSLY
Acts 4:5-31

The next morning the Jewish rulers and the high priest and his family met together at Jerusalem. The rulers, dressed in their long robes, sat in a half circle, as was the custom.

Show Illustration #4

Then Peter and John were brought in from the jail. The healed man was there too, and stood with them in the center of the group.

The rulers asked, "By whose power, or by what name have you done this?"

Peter, filled with the Holy Spirit, spoke boldly: "You rulers of the people, if we are being tried today for a good deed done to this man who was helpless and you want to know how he was made well, I will tell you. It was done through the name of Jesus Christ, whom you crucified. But God raised Him from the dead and by Him this man is standing before you well and strong. And there is no salvation through any other person. There is no other name in all the world–but the name of Jesus–given among men, through whom we must be saved!"

The rulers couldn't believe what they were hearing. How could these uneducated, untrained fishermen speak so well–and so boldly? The rulers recognized that these were men who had been with Jesus. And there was no use arguing against miracles, for the man who had been healed was standing there with them.

So they ordered Peter and John to leave the room. Then they discussed among themselves: "What shall we do to these men? We cannot deny that a great miracle has been done by them. Everyone living in Jerusalem knows about it. But we must keep the news of this from spreading any further. Let us warn them never again to speak to anyone in this name of Jesus."

So they called for Peter and John and commanded them, "You are not to speak nor teach again in the name of Jesus!"

Did Peter and John make the promise? They did not! Instead they answered the rulers: "Which is right in the sight of God, to listen to you or to obey God? For we cannot stop speaking about the things which we have seen and heard."

What could the rulers say to that? They did not know how they could punish them because of the people. For the people were praising God for all that had happened. So the rulers threatened both men and let them go.

Peter and John were free! They hurried to tell their friends what the rulers had said. When they heard the story, they all prayed together saying, "Lord, Thou art God. You have made Heaven and earth and the sea and all that is in them. And now, Lord, hear the threats of the rulers and give us, Your servants, courage to speak Your Word without fear. Cause signs and wonders to be done in the name of Your holy servant, Jesus."

When they finished praying, the building shook. And they were all filled with the Holy Spirit and they spoke the Word of God courageously, exactly as they had prayed they would. God had answered their prayer.

Are you willing to tell others about the Lord Jesus even if you might have to suffer for it? If people laugh at you, will you still be a bold witness? Do not be afraid to suffer for Christ's sake. (See John 15:18, 24; 1 John 3:13.)

Today we have learned that Christians–even those who do the perfect will of God–sometimes have to suffer. But our Bible memory verse reminds us of something that should help us in our suffering for the Lord Jesus. It is this: ". . . The sufferings of this present time are not worthy to be compared with the glory which shall be revealed in us." In other words, whatever we have to go through now is nothing compared with the glorious future God has planned for us. Think of that!

Lesson 2
IN PRISON FOR CHRIST'S SAKE

Scripture to be studied: Acts 5:12-42

The *aim* of the lesson: To show there can be real joy in suffering for Jesus Christ.

What your students should *know*: It is only the power of God in their lives that can make them rejoice in their problems.

What your students should *feel*: A desire to rejoice instead of complain when problems come.

What your students should *do*: Ask God to fill their hearts with peace and joy when troubles come.

Lesson outline (for the teacher's and students' notebooks):
1. The sick are healed in the name of Jesus (Acts 5:12-16).
2. The apostles imprisoned for serving the Lord (Acts 5:17-20).
3. The apostles preach the Gospel to the rulers (Acts 5:21-39).
4. The apostles rejoice, though suffering and in disgrace (Acts 5:40-42).

The verse to be memorized:

For I reckon that the sufferings of this present time are not worthy to be compared with the glory which shall be revealed in us. (Romans 8:18)

NOTE TO THE TEACHER

In our last lesson we taught that Christians, even those in the will of God, *can* and *do* suffer. In this lesson we see that there can be real joy in suffering for Jesus Christ. May the Lord give you joy, dear teacher, as you teach this lesson.

May your heart be thrilled as you see how God used something as insignificant as the shadow of Peter to show His power. Surely He is willing and ready to fill you with His mighty power and use you in ways you never dreamed possible as you yield yourself to Him. Do not let opposition of any kind stop you. Follow the advice of Paul who wrote: "Rejoice in the Lord always; and again I say rejoice" (Philippians 4:4). And remember that Paul wrote that when he was in prison!

THE LESSON

Peter and John had been warned by the men of the council before whom they had been on trial: "Do not talk to anyone in the name of Jesus." (See Acts 4:17-18.)

But none of the apostles could keep quiet about their faith in the Lord Jesus. The warnings and threats of their enemies did not stop these men of God, even though Peter and John had already spent time in prison for speaking about Jesus. They all wanted to tell others the news that was too good to keep to themselves. Their own lives had been changed through Jesus Christ and the power of the Holy Spirit. Now they wanted to share their joy with the entire world so that men and women and children everywhere could know the truth about Jesus Christ–that He had died for their sins and that He had risen from the dead. How could people believe in Jesus if they did not hear about Him?

Many did hear and multitudes believed in Jesus as Peter preached day after day in the part of the temple known as Solomon's Porch. Lives were changed and the Church of Jesus Christ grew.

1. THE SICK ARE HEALED IN THE NAME OF JESUS
Acts 5:12-16

Show Illustration #5

Wonderful things took place every day. Sick people were brought to the apostles to be healed. It didn't matter whether they were lame or blind or deaf. It didn't matter if every doctor in Jerusalem had said that these people could not be healed. Though every medicine had failed to make these helpless ones well, they were healed by the power of God. Many of them were carried to the streets and placed on beds or couches so that, if Peter came by, his shadow would pass over them–and they'd be healed. It was not the shadow that had cured them–it was God's great power. Sick bodies were made well, demons were cast out, lives were changed–all in the name of Jesus Christ.

2. THE APOSTLES IMPRISONED FOR SERVING THE LORD
Acts 5:17-20

When the high priest heard about it, he was furious. The apostles had not obeyed him. They were continuing to preach and to heal people in the name of Jesus. It would have been a different matter if the apostles had made the sick well in the name of the high priest. That would have made the high priest happy. But he was jealous. The people were listening to Peter and John instead of to him. If only the crowds would gather around him instead of the apostles! If only his name had the same power as the name of Jesus!

The Sadducees, too, were angry. They did not believe in miracles. They did not believe that Jesus had risen from the grave. How then could they explain what the apostles were doing? How could the name of Jesus be so powerful if Jesus was still dead?

The religious leaders decided that something had to be done quickly. So they arrested all twelve apostles and put them into prison. Later they would decide what they must do to keep them from ever again talking about Jesus.

Show Illustration #6

So it was that Peter and John and James and Philip and Nathanael and all the other apostles were arrested and locked in prison. Strong guards stood in front of the doors to see that the apostles could not escape.

But God was watching and caring for His children. He had a plan for the apostles. There was more work for them to do–more teaching, more preaching. That night, when all was quiet, God sent his angel to open the prison doors. No key was needed. Not a sound was made as the angel opened the great doors and led the apostles outside. The guards neither saw nor heard what was happening.

The angel told the apostles, "Go back to the temple and preach about this new life."

– 21 –

3. THE APOSTLES PREACH THE GOSPEL TO THE RULERS
Acts 5:21-39

The next morning the high priest and all the rulers of the Sanhedrin had a meeting to decide what to do with the apostles. They sent to the prison to have the apostles brought to them. Soon the officers rushed back with the shocking news: "The prisoners have escaped! We cannot find them!"

Show Illustration #7

The men of the Sanhedrin stared at the officers who had brought this astonishing news. Could it be possible that all the apostles had escaped?

The officers explained: "When we got to the prison, we found all the doors locked. The guards were standing there. But when we looked inside, the prisoners were not there. Not one of them!"

When the high priest and the captain of the temple and the other rulers heard this, they were troubled. What could have happened? Where were the apostles?

Right then someone came in and announced: "The men whom you put in prison are now back in the temple, standing there teaching the people!"

It did not seem possible. "Bring them here at once," was the order.

As the officers hurried away, the captain of the temple went with them. "You had better be careful," he warned the officers. "If you are rough with these men, the people will be angry. They will stone you."

When the captain and the officers marched into the temple they found the apostles teaching just as if nothing had happened. Quickly, but without any violence, the officers arrested them again and led them out of the temple and back to the hall where the rulers were waiting.

As the apostles stood before the council, the high priest cried, "We gave you strict orders not to teach in the name of Jesus. And what have you done? You have filled Jerusalem with your teaching and you are blaming us for the death of Jesus."

Then Peter and the other apostles answered courageously, "We must obey God rather than men. The God of our fathers raised Jesus from the dead. He is the one you put to death by hanging Him on a cross. But God raised Him as Prince and Saviour to give forgiveness of sins. And we are witnesses of these things, and so is the Holy Spirit whom God has given to all who obey Him."

These bold words made the rulers so angry that they wanted to have the apostles put to death. But one of the council members, a man named Gamaliel, stood up and asked that the apostles be taken out of the room. Gamaliel was a wise man and respected by all the people. When the apostles had been taken away he said, "You men of Israel, be careful what you do with these men. Some time ago there was a man named Theudeus who pretended to be someone great. About 400 men joined him. But he was killed and all of his followers were scattered. That was the end of that group.

"Then there was another man called Judas from Galilee. Many people followed him. But he, too, died and all his followers were scattered.

"Now I am telling you to leave these apostles alone. If their teaching is from themselves alone, nothing will come of it. It will pass away. But if it is of God, you cannot overthrow it. You could find yourselves fighting against God."

The council decided that Gamaliel had given good advice. So they called the apostles back to the room.

4. THE APOSTLES REJOICE, THOUGH SUFFERING AND IN DISGRACE
Acts 5:40-42

Show Illustration #8

First they had them whipped, just as if they were criminals. They ordered them never again to speak in the name of Jesus. Then they set them free.

As the apostles left the council their backs were sore from the whippings. We would expect them to be depressed and defeated. Instead, they sent from the presence of those Jewish rulers full of joy. They rejoiced that God had considered them worthy to suffer disgrace for the name of Jesus.

Where did the apostles go after the warnings and beatings? Back to the temple! Every day, in the temple and in the homes they continued to teach and preach about Jesus Christ.

The apostles had not escaped suffering. But God gave them such joy and power that they were able to rejoice in their trials. They welcomed every difficulty. (Read James 1:2; 1 Peter 4:12-13.) Jesus had suffered much for them; now they had the privilege of suffering for Him.

It is one thing to *have* to suffer. It is another thing to he *willing* to suffer. And it is quite another thing to be *glad* to suffer. Only the power of the Holy Spirit in our lives can make us rejoice in our problems.

When difficulties, trials, problems, troubles come into your life, do you complain? Or do you ask God to fill your life with His peace and to fill your heart with rejoicing? When you, as a Christian, are called upon to suffer for Christ, remember that the suffering is just for a little while and the very best things are yet to come.

Lesson 3
DEATH FOR CHRIST'S SAKE

Scripture to be studied: Acts 6-7

The *aim* of the lesson: To show that Jesus knows about and understands all our suffering for Him.

> **What your students should *know*:** Stephen never once turned away from the Lord Jesus while he was suffering.
>
> **What your students should *feel*:** A desire to be a bold witness for Christ.
>
> **What your students should *do*:** Ask God to help them face problems–even death–as Stephen did.

Lesson outline (for the teacher's and students' notebooks):

1. Stephen and six others chosen to care for the poor (Acts 6:1-7).
2. Stephen is falsely accused (Acts 6:8-15).
3. Stephen boldly proclaims Christ (Acts 7:1-56).
4. Stephen asks God to forgive those who stoned him to death (Acts 7:57-60).

The verse to be memorized:

> *For I reckon that the sufferings of this present time are not worthy to be compared with the glory which shall be revealed in us.* (Romans 8:18)

NOTE TO THE TEACHER

It has been said that persecution does not make a man willing to die for his faith; it simply reveals those who already have that kind of faith. Stephen was this kind of man. He was the first Christian to seal his testimony with his blood.

The experience of Stephen reveals to us that Jesus Christ sees, knows and understands our suffering. He cares about us and sympathizes. No one understands like Jesus.

When we see Christ in our sufferings and sorrows, we can have victory and peace. His grace is sufficient for every trial no matter how severe. The blessed hope of the coming of the Lord is a comfort to the suffering believer.

THE LESSON
1. STEPHEN AND SIX OTHERS CHOSEN TO CARE FOR THE POOR
Acts 6:1-7

The twelve apostles were busy. Every day they prayed and preached and taught the people the Word of God. They also took care of distributing needful things to the poor.

But as the Church continued to grow, there was too much for the apostles to do. Some of the people began to feel neglected.

At that time most of the believers were Jews who had been born in Judea and who spoke the Hebrew language. But there were some believers who were Jews who had been born outside Judea and who spoke Greek. They were called Greek Jews.

Show Illustration #9

One day some of the Greek Jews came to the apostles and said, "You have not been fair. You are not giving as much food and care to the Greek Jewish widows as you are to the others."

The apostles were troubled. They did not want problems among the members of the Church. They wanted to be fair. It was important for the believers to get along well together.

So the apostles called the Christians together and spoke to them about the problem. "It would not be good for us to spend less time in teaching the Word of God and to spend more time in sitting at tables and distributing money for food and clothing for the needy. And yet the widows need to be fed and cared for. We have decided that you should choose seven of your own men who are honest and who have a good reputation. These men should also be full of the Holy Spirit and wisdom. When you have made your choice, we shall appoint the seven men to do this important work of feeding the poor. Then we shall give ourselves whole heartedly to prayer and to the ministry of the Word of God."

The believers were pleased with the suggestion. They chose seven men to take charge of the gifts, to see that they were given equally to those in need.

The first man chosen was Stephen. His name meant "crown." Stephen and the other six men were brought before the apostles, who laid their hands on them, prayed for them and set them apart to care for the poor in the Church.

The problem had been solved. And, because the apostles were busy teaching, the Word of God continued to spread. As a result, multitudes in Jerusalem believed in the Lord Jesus Christ.

2. STEPHEN IS FALSELY ACCUSED
Acts 6:8-15

But more trouble came to the Church. This is what happened: Stephen was a man of great faith and was filled with the Spirit of God. He did more than look after the needy ones. He also preached the Gospel of Christ and did great wonders and miracles among the people. Some of the Jews who heard Stephen preach did not agree with what he said. So they argued with him. But, no matter what they said, Stephen always had a wise and powerful answer. This made the men very angry. They did not know how to silence Stephen. They hated him and they hated the Lord Jesus of whom he spoke.

Show Illustration #10

Then these wicked men stirred up the people against Stephen. They brought in some men to say things that were not true. "We have heard Stephen speak against Moses and against God," they lied.

When the people heard this, they seized Stephen and brought him to the council. Once again they called in false witnesses to accuse this man of God. They shouted, "This man will not stop talking against our holy temple and against the Law. We have heard him say that Jesus will destroy this temple and will change the customs which have come down to us from Moses."

As the liars spoke, the men of the council fixed their eyes on Stephen. Was he worried or afraid? No! Instead his face glowed like that of an angel.

– 23 –

3. STEPHEN BOLDLY PROCLAIMS CHRIST
Acts 7:1-56

Then the high priest asked, "Are these things true that have been said about you?"

Stephen, with the light of God showing on his face, began to speak, not for one minute or two or even five. He talked on and on. He told of the great things that God had done for the people of Israel in the past; how He had called Abraham and Isaac and Jacob and had blessed them. He told of Moses and of his wisdom and might in words and deeds. He told how Moses had been called by God to be a deliverer of the people of Israel.

Then Stephen said boldly, "But our fathers would not obey God. They turned instead to a calf-god made of gold, offering sacrifices to it."

The council listened. They knew that everything Stephen said was true. But he was not finished speaking. With great courage he said to the council members: "You stubborn and hard-hearted people, you do not obey the Holy Spirit. You have done just as your fathers did. Your fathers persecuted the prophets and killed those who told about the coming of the Just One, Jesus. And now you have betrayed and killed Jesus."

Show Illustration #11

The council became furious at Stephen. They ground their teeth in rage. But Stephen, full of the Holy Spirit, looked up steadily into Heaven and saw the glory of God and saw Jesus standing–standing at the right hand of God. Then Stephen exclaimed, "Look! I see the heavens opened, and the Son of Man standing at the right hand of God."

4. STEPHEN ASKS GOD TO FORGIVE THOSE WHO STONED HIM TO DEATH
Acts 7:57-60

Show Illustration #12

The council could not bear any more. They shouted loudly and held their hands over their ears. Then they grabbed Stephen and dragged him from the council room, down the street and out of the city. There they flung large, heavy stones at Stephen. Those who were throwing the stones tossed their coats at the feet of a young man–named Saul–who agreed that Stephen should die.

As the men hurled stones, Stephen prayed, "Lord Jesus, receive my spirit." He knew that though these men killed his body they could not destroy him. He knew that soon he would enter into the very presence of Jesus whom he saw standing at the right hand of God. He knew that Jesus was watching over him and that He understood and cared. In his suffering, Stephen was not alone. He had the Lord Jesus to help him and give him joy and peace and strength.

As more stones were thrown at him, Stephen cried with a loud voice, "Lord, forgive them for this sin."

When he had said this, Stephen died. His bruised and beaten body lay dead. But Stephen went immediately to be with Jesus Christ, the One for whom he had suffered and died.

Nothing made Stephen turn back from his love for the Lord Jesus. Nothing kept him from telling others of that love, even though it meant suffering and death.

While Stephen was suffering, Jesus Christ was watching. Although He is usually *seated* in Heaven (see Hebrews 10:12), when He saw Stephen suffering, He *stood*.

Whenever you suffer for the Lord Jesus, remember that He is watching–oh, so carefully. He understands because He suffered more than anyone has ever suffered. He loves you very much and He will never forsake you. Remember, too, that your trials, your problems, your difficulties will not last forever. "The sufferings of this present time are not worthy to be compared with the glory which shall be revealed in us" (Romans 8:18).

Lesson 4
SUFFERING IS COMMON TO ALL MANKIND

NOTE TO THE TEACHER
Volumes 14 through 18 of *The Visualized Bible Series* deal with lessons in the book of Acts. In this sixteenth volume the first three lessons deal with some of the suffering the apostles experienced–the kind that witnessing Christians sometimes have to endure today. However, believers in Christ, as well as unbelievers, suffer in other ways. So, before leaving this particular subject, we want to look at another Bible book which clearly teaches that suffering is a part of life for mankind generally. Job was probably one of the first books of the Bible to be written. The trials and sufferings, which came into the life of Job, may come into the life of anyone.

While it is important to know *how* people of God have suffered, it is even more important to learn *why* they suffered. So we shall discuss the *reasons* for suffering and the *rewards* for suffering. (We trust that your students are making careful notes in their notebooks.)

Scripture to be studied: Job 1, 2, 42

The *aim* of the lesson: To show why people suffer.

What your students should *know*: When they get to Heaven they will understand why they are suffering now.

What your students should *feel*: A desire to suffer gladly for Christ.

What your students should *do*: Trust the Lord Jesus to give strength for each new problem.

Lesson outline (for the teacher's and students' notebooks):
1. Almost everything Job had is destroyed (Job 1:1–2:10).
2. Some suffering is caused by sin (Job 2:11-13).
3. Job listens to God, forgives his unkind friends and receives God's blessing (Job 38:1–42:15).
4. Jesus Christ suffered and so shall we (Luke 24:46; Romans 8:18).

The verse to be memorized:

For I reckon that the sufferings of this present time are not worthy to be compared with the glory which shall be revealed in us. (Romans 8:18)

THE LESSON

All through the years many have asked the question, "Why do good people suffer?" We can understand that sometimes people who are evil are punished. But why do godly men and women have to suffer?

1. ALMOST EVERYTHING JOB HAD IS DESTROYED
Job 1:1–2:10

Hundreds of years before the apostles lived, there was a good man who suffered greatly. And he wondered why. The name of this man was Job. He lived in the land of Uz near the Arabian Desert. He had a wife, seven sons and three daughters. He owned thousands of sheep, camels, oxen, donkeys and had many servants. Job was the greatest of all men in the East.

Show Illustration #13

One day this godly man received some terrifying news. In fact there seemed to be no end to the bad news. Messengers rushed in one after the other to tell Job about the sudden and fearful events that were taking place.

"Your oxen and donkeys have been stolen by the Sabeans and your servants have been killed!" one messenger exclaimed.

"Lightning has killed your sheep!" another announced.

Still another told him, "The Chaldeans stole all your camels!"

Then a messenger came with the worst news of all: "A whirlwind knocked down your son's house and killed all your children."

How could so many awful things happen to one man in one day? But that was not the end. Only a short time later Job became very sick with painful boils and sores all over his body. He went outside and sat down on a heap of ashes. His wife told him, "Curse God and die."

But Job answered, "You are speaking like a foolish woman. Shall we receive good things from the hand of God, and shall we not receive evil?" Job refused to talk against God no matter what happened to him.

What Job did not realize was that it was Satan, the enemy of God, who had brought these terrible things upon him. Satan wanted to prove that Job would not love and worship God if all of his possessions were taken from him.

2. SOME SUFFERING IS CAUSED BY SIN
Job 2:11-13

As Job sat in the ashes, three friends came to see him. They wept at the sight of Job. They sat down with him. But not one of them spoke. For seven days and nights they sat on the ground with Job–but they never said a word. Finally, when they did speak, they said things that did not help Job at all. They told him that he was suffering because of his sins. They said that if a person suffered greatly it was because he must be a great sinner.

But Job insisted that he had not done any great sin. He had tried his best to please God, he said.

Show Illustration #14

By this time a fourth man, named Elihu, arrived. He was angry with the other three men for the way they talked to Job. He did not agree that suffering is always punishment for sin. He was also annoyed with Job for having said he was not a sinner. Elihu explained that he believed that suffering is sent upon men to keep them from sinning. He believed that a good man like Job could become an even better man through suffering.

Elihu was right. It is true that some people have to suffer punishment because of their sins. It is also true that through suffering men may be kept from sinning. But there was more to know about suffering than even Elihu understood.

3. JOB LISTENS TO GOD, FORGIVES HIS UNKIND FRIENDS AND RECEIVES GOD'S BLESSING
Job 38:1–42:15

Show Illustration #15

The next voice Job heard was the voice of God. The voice came to him out of a whirlwind. God asked Job sixty questions, one after the other. Some of these questions were: "Where were you when I laid the foundations of the earth?" "Can you lift your voice up to the clouds to cause the rain to fall?" "Can you send lightning?" "Did you give the peacocks their beautiful feathers?" "Did you give wings or feathers to the ostrich?"

Job listened to question after question. He knew that God alone could do those wonderful things. He began to realize how very great God is and how very little man is. Also, he saw that God is perfect and right and that man, even the most righteous man on earth, is sinful.

Job had one answer: "Behold, I am vile; what shall I answer Thee? I will lay my hand upon my mouth." Job knew he was a sinner before God. He realized, too, that God knew everything and could do everything. God, the Creator of the universe, knows man better than man knows himself. If God allows a man to suffer, then suffering is right for that man, even though he cannot understand it.

But the story of Job does not end there. After Job confessed that he was a sinner, he began to pray for the friends who had said such unkind things to him during his suffering. Then the Lord took away his sickness and gave him twice as many possessions as he had had before. The Lord gave him many more thousands of sheep and camels and oxen and donkeys. He also gave him seven more sons and three more daughters who were the most beautiful women in all the land. So the Lord blessed Job more at the end of his life than at the beginning. That is the way God does things. For every child of God, the best is still to come.

4. JESUS CHRIST SUFFERED AND SO SHALL WE
Luke 24:46; Romans 8:18

The lessons Job learned are lessons for all of us. But there is One who suffered even more than Job suffered. Can you tell who He is? Yes, the Lord Jesus Christ.

Show Illustration #16

It was one thing for God to look down from Heaven and see His people suffer; it was quite another thing for Him to look down and see His own dear Son suffer. That which Jesus suffered on the cross could never fully be described. But He suffered many other things before that time–poverty, loneliness, heartache, hatred, misunderstanding, homelessness, betrayal.

Because we trust God, we also should be willing to accept the trials, the problems, the difficulties which He allows. Peter suffered gladly for Jesus Christ. So did the other apostles. Others have suffered, not necessarily because of their witness for Christ, but in the same way that all men suffer as a result of Adam's sin. Thus all through the years many have experienced poverty, loneliness, sickness, pain, loss of honor, loss of property, loss of friends and untimely death.

Perhaps you are wondering what good there is in suffering. You will remember the facts better if you list them in your notebook under this heading:

1. Suffering can bring glory to God. (See Acts 4:21.)
   The Christian is a witness for God. Suffering Christians show others the peace and comfort and joy that God alone can give. (See John 14:27; 15:11; 2 Corinthians 1:3.)
2. God sometimes uses suffering to discipline His children. (See Hebrews 12:3-15.)
   Because He loves us very much, God wants us to be in the very center of His will. When we disobey and begin to wander from His path, He disciplines us to bring us back to Himself.
3. We learn obedience through suffering. (See Hebrews 5:8; Philippians 2:8.)
   Through suffering we become more dependent upon God and He gently draws us to Himself. The Christian soon learns that God wants His children to be obedient.
4. Suffering keeps us from becoming proud. (See 2 Corinthians 12:7.) Sometimes God has to deal with His children to humble them. Suffering makes us depend more upon God and less upon ourselves.
5. Suffering teaches us faith and trust. (See 1 Peter 1:7-8.)
   When a Christian suffers he finds that there is no one–apart from God–who can fully understand and sympathize. Through suffering we learn to cast our cares entirely upon God. (See 1 Peter 5:7.)
6. Suffering teaches us how to comfort others. (See 2 Corinthians 1:4.)
   Now that we have seen six reasons why a Christian should be willing to suffer, let us look at the very best part of all:

Do you remember the memory verse? Let us say it together: "For I reckon that the sufferings of this present time are not worthy to be compared with the glory which shall be revealed in us" (Romans 8:18).

Ever since you and I received Jesus Christ as our Saviour, we have belonged to God. His home–Heaven–has become our home. (See Hebrews 13:14.) And yet we still remain on this earth as witnesses for Jesus Christ. We still live in these earthly bodies–bodies that suffer and die. But one of these days God is going to give us new bodies. (See 2 Corinthians 5:1-10.) When Jesus Christ returns we will all be changed in a moment. Our new, heavenly bodies will never have to suffer or die. In that wonderful day the children of God will not only see the glory of Christ, but they will share in that glory for they will be glorified with Him. (See Hebrews 2:10; Romans 8:29-30.)

In Heaven, God will have surprises and rewards for faithful Christians who have suffered for Him–rewards such as you have never dreamed of. (See 2 Corinthians 4:17-18.) Our trials (which pass quickly) are winning for us a permanent, glorious reward out of all proportion to our problems. There, in Heaven, we will see for ourselves how all things–the dark things, the sad things, the bitter things–have worked together for good to those who love God. (See Romans 8:28.)

So be glad. Walk on. Keep looking to Jesus until that day when we see His glorious face. Then we will not even remember the sufferings of this earth. We will enjoy eternal joy and satisfaction forever and ever.

www.ingramcontent.com/pod-product-compliance
Lightning Source LLC
Chambersburg PA
CBHW060805090426
42736CB00002B/164